SUPERMAN ADVENTURES

Raintree

Raintree is an imprint of Capstone
Global Library Limited, a company
incorporated in England and Wales
having its registered office at
7 Pilgrim Street, London, EC4V
6LB - Registered company number:
6695582

To contact Raintree please phone
0845 6044371, fax + 44 (0) 1865
312263, or email myorders@
raintreepublishers.co.uk.
Customers from outside the UK
please telephone +44 1865 312262.

Originally published by DC Comics in the U.S. in single magazine
form as Superman Adventures #7.
Copyright © 2013 DC Comics. All Rights Reserved.

DC Comics
1700 Broadway, New York, NY 10019
A Warner Bros. Entertainment Company

First published by Stone Arch Books in 2013
First published in the United Kingdom in 2014
The moral rights of the proprietor have been asserted.

Ashley C. Andersen Zantop *Publisher*
Michael Dahl *Editorial Director*
Donald Lemke & Sean Tulien *Editors*
Heather Kindseth *Creative Director*
Bob Lentz *Designer*
Kathy McColley *Production Specialist*

DC COMICS
Mike McAvennie *Original US Editor*
Rick Burchett & Terry Austin *Cover Artists*

Originated by Capstone Global Library Ltd
Printed and bound in China by Leo Paper
Products Ltd

ISBN 978 1 406 26682 5
17 16 15 14 13
10 9 8 7 6 5 4 3 2 1

British Library Cataloguing in Publication Data
A full catalogue record for this book is available
from the British Library.

SUPERMAN ADVENTURES

Tiny Problems!

Scott McCloud...................... writer
Rick Burchett ....penciller
Terry Austin .... inker
Marie Severin .... colourist
Lois Buhalis....................... letterer

Superman created by
Jerry Siegel & Joe Shuster

SCOTT McCLOUD - BIG WORDS • RICK BURCHETT - PETITE PENCILS • TERRY AUSTIN - IMMENSE INKS • LOIS BUHALIS - LI'L LETTERS • MARIE SEVERIN - COLOSSAL COLORS • MIKE McAVENNIE - HALF-PINT

SUPERMAN CREATED BY JERRY SIEGEL & JOE SHUSTER

SO, SUPERMAN, WHY DIDN'T YOU JUST LEAVE THEM IN THE *PHANTOM ZONE?* ISN'T THAT WHERE THE KRYPTONIAN GOVERN-MENT *EXILED* THEM WHEN THEY TRIED TO STAGE THAT COUP?

THAT'S TRUE, LOIS, BUT THEY'VE BEEN LEFT TO *OUR* LAWS NOW, AND BELIEVE ME-- THE PHANTOM ZONE IS THE VERY *DEFINITION* OF *CRUEL AND UNUSUAL PUNISHMENT.*

FOR ALL HIS BLUSTER, I'M SURE OUR LITTLE GENERAL WOULD PREFER *ANY* HUMILIATION TO RETURNING THERE.

≥*Hmph!*≤ I'D HAVE LEFT THEM THERE FOR GOOD.

SO WHAT ARE THEIR CHANCES OF REHABILITATION?

GOOD QUESTION. GENERAL, WHAT ARE THE CHANCES··?

NEVER!!

PROFESSOR HAMILTON, IS YOUR DEMONSTRATION READY?

YES. ≥*Ahem*≤ AS YOU CAN SEE, THE PROCESS IS SIMPLE ENOUGH. OUR *MOLECULAR SCALING GENERATOR* CAN TAKE ANY OBJECT--LIKE THIS *BASKETBALL*--

--AND REDUCE IT TO AS LITTLE AS *ONE ONE-HUNDREDTH* OF ITS PREVIOUS SIZE.

7

WITH SOME ADJUSTMENTS WE'LL BE MAKING BACK AT *S.T.A.R. LABS*, WE CAN ALSO RESTORE THOSE SAME OBJECTS TO THEIR PREVIOUS SIZE.

OF COURSE, WE'LL NEED TO KEEP THE GENERATOR ON-GROUNDS, IN CASE THERE ARE ANY PROBLEMS.

I'VE HEARD *ENOUGH!* HOW DO WE KNOW THIS FLIMSY LITTLE CAGE CAN *HOLD* 'EM?

SO EVEN IF THEY *DO* BREAK OUT OF THEIR "CAGE," INSPECTOR, THESE CHEMICALLY-COATED CELL WALLS WILL PREVENT ALL SUNLIGHT FROM ENTERING THE ROOM.

THEY'LL *STILL* FIND A WAY OUT. THEY'RE NOT STUPID.

IN THIS STATE, THEY'L BE AS EASY T CONTAIN AS ANY *HUMAN* INSPECTOR.

EASY, DAN. THE PROFESSOR SAYS THEY WON'T HAVE ANY POWERS AS LONG AS THEY DON'T RECEIVE ANY OF OUR YELLOW SUNLIGHT.

"*HUMAN*"? YOU DARE COMPARE US TO *HUMANS*? I WON'T *TOLERATE* SUCH AN INSULT!

I'LL TAKE ANY HUMAN OVER *YOU*, YOU MURDERING LITTLE *FREAKS!*

DAN, C'MON. ENOUGH.

WHETHER YOU ADMIT IT OR NOT, JAX-UR, WE'RE DOING YOU A FAVOR. I SUGGEST YOU LEARN TO *APPRECIATE* IT.

IN ANY EVENT, YOU'RE HERE TO STAY.

WELL, INSPECTOR, IT APPEARS YOU GOT A GOOD WORKOUT.

THESE HOODS NEVER LEARN.

LOOKS LIKE YOU KNOCKED SOME SENSE INTO THEM, DAN.

OKAY, LOOKS LIKE MINIMUM DAMAGE, WARDEN. JUST SOME CEILING REPAIR IN CELL BLOCKS EIGHT THROUGH TEN.

EIGHT THROUGH TEN?!

HEY, HOLD ON! IT'S NOTHING SERIOUS! JUST SOME CRACKS, A FEW HOLES...

NOTHING ANYONE COULD *ESCAPE* THROUGH.

AND NOTHING'S GETTING IN--

--BUT A LITTLE *SUNLIGHT.*

14

:OOF!:

SOMEBODY STOP--

--THEM.

:OMPH!:

Ha-ha-ha!

:Unnh!:

WHUDD!

FAREWELL, FOOLS!

'TIL WE MEET AGAIN!

Huh--?

:Unnh!:

YOU KNOW, TURPIN, YOU MIGHT WANT TO START COUNTING YOUR CALORIES.

THE NEXT MORNING.

HEY, RON, HAVE YOU SEEN KENT THIS MORNING?

NO, LOIS. HE'S NOT IN YET.

AND HE MISSED HIS MEETING WITH PERRY THIS MORNING.

Hunh. THAT'S NOT LIKE HIM.

HI, LOIS. COULD YOU TELL PERRY I CAN'T MAKE IT THIS MORNING? I CAME DOWN WITH THE FLU. THANKS. SEE YOU TOMORROW, HOPEFULLY.

click

OH, GREAT-- NOW I'VE GOT TO FILE THAT PAPERWORK BY MYSEL--

LOIS!

Hunh? WAS THAT A VOICE?

LOIS! LOIS, IT'S ME!

DOWN HERE!

!

16

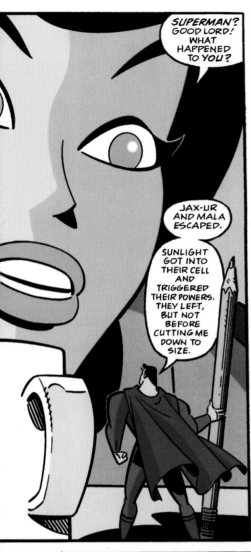

SUPERMAN? *GOOD LORD!* WHAT HAPPENED TO *YOU?*

JAX-UR AND MALA ESCAPED.

SUNLIGHT GOT INTO THEIR CELL AND TRIGGERED THEIR POWERS. THEY LEFT, BUT NOT BEFORE CUTTING ME DOWN TO SIZE.

NOW THAT THEY'VE HAD A DAY IN THE SUN, THEY'LL BE AT FULL POWER. AND THOSE POWERS ARE ARE NOW *PERMANENT* LIKE MINE!

HAMILTON SAID HE *COULD* REVERSE THE EFFECTS OF THE SIZE-CHANGER...

ES, AND JAX-UR AND MALA EARD HIM. I CALLED THE ROFESSOR FIRST THING. E'S IN TRANSIT NOW. VEN *I* DON'T KNOW WHERE HE IS.

UT I'VE TOLD HIM O RENDEZVOUS WITH E AT YOUR APART-ENT. HOPE YOU DON'T MIND.

WELL, YOU KNOW, THE ROYAL FAMILY *WAS* COMING OVER TONIGHT, BUT--

YEAH, OF *COURSE* IT'S FINE. WHAT TIME?

7:30, AND IT-- *WAIT.* SOMEBODY'S COMING.

LOIS, HAVE YOU SEEN KENT THIS MORNING?

SORRY, PERRY, HE'S OUT WITH THE FLU.

Oh, *GREAT*-- *ANOTHER* CASUALTY.

RON, WAIT--I'VE GOT A JOB FOR YOU.

WHILE WE'RE WAITING, WHY DON'T YOU CHECK THE WIRES TO SEE IF THERE'S ANY NEWS OF *TWO-INCH-HIGH ALIENS* CAUSING TROUBLE?

I'LL TRY, BUT SOMETHING TELLS ME THE A.P. MIGHT NOT CARRY A STORY LIKE THAT, EVEN IF IT *IS* TRUE.

NOW IF ONLY THE *NATIONAL WHISPER* HAD A WIRE SERVICE...

QUITTING TIME.

YaaaWWNN STILL NOTHING. I GUESS WE'D BETTER HEAD BACK TO THE APARTMENT.

BETTER PUT ME IN YOUR HANDBAG.

WE'RE TRYING TO KEEP MY CONDITION A SECRET. IF INTERGANG KNEW ABOUT THIS, THEY'D HAVE A FIELD DAY!

YOU *SEE*, MY PET? OUR PATIENCE WILL BEAR FRUIT YET.

LOIS, DON'T TELL ME YOU'RE *LEAVING.* PERRY WILL HAVE A *FIT!*

NO CHOICE, RON. FAMILY EMERGENCY.

SORRY ABOUT THE MESS.

I DON'T KNOW WHERE ALL THIS JUNK COMES FROM.

YOU SHOULD SEE *CLARK KENT'S* APARTMENT. SO CLEAN IT LOOKS LIKE A *MUSEUM.*

I *LIKE* YOURS, LOIS. IT LOOKS... *LIVED-IN.*

Ding-Dong!

MISS LANE.

PROFESSOR. WANT TO DO TAKE-OUT CHINESE OR PIZZA?

I BEG YOUR PARDON?

LET'S JUST GET *STARTED,* SHALL WE?

SUPERMAN, *CAREFUL!* YOU'RE HEADING FOR--

--*YOW!* SORRY, AUNT GLADYS!

THWAKK!

SKRASH!

HEY, *LOOK OUT!* MY NICE NEW GLASS...

SKRASSH!

...COFFEE TABLE.

LISTEN, YOU *CREEPS!* IF YOU *DON'T* GET OUT OF MY APARTMENT, I'M GONNA--

YOU'RE GOING TO *WHAT*, HUMAN?

THIS!

ARRGH!

FWUMP!

SMAK!

I'LL *RIP* YOU APART FOR THAT, WOMAN!

-STARTING WITH SOME *HOUSEHOLD PESTS!*

≈WHEW≈ WHEN YOU'RE IN A CLEANING MOOD...

PSSSST!

YAAAAR!

UH-OH... EMPTY.

shhk-shhk!

YOU-- *--YOU--!*

RAAAR!

MM!

DON'T INSULT OUR HOST, MALA!

UH-OH, SUPERMAN, WAIT, WAIT--

KTHOKK

--NOT THE--

SKASSH!

--VASE.

23

CREATORS

SCOTT McCLOUD *WRITER*

Scott McCloud is an acclaimed comics creator and author whose best-known work is the graphic novel *Understanding Comics*. His work also includes the science-fiction adventure series *Zot!*, a 12-issue run of *Superman Adventures*, and much more. Scott is the creator of the "24 Hour Comic", and frequently lectures on comics theory.

RICK BURCHETT *PENCILLER*

Rick Burchett has worked as a comics artist for more than 25 years. He has received the comics industry's Eisner Award three times, Spain's Haxtur Award, and he has been nominated for the Eagle Award in the UK. Rick lives with his wife and two sons in Missouri, USA.

TERRY AUSTIN *INKER*

Throughout his career, inker Terry Austin has received dozens of awards for his work on high-profile comics for DC Comics and Marvel, such as *The Uncanny X-Men*, *Doctor Strange*, *Justice League America*, *Green Lantern*, and *Superman Adventures*. He lives in New York, USA.

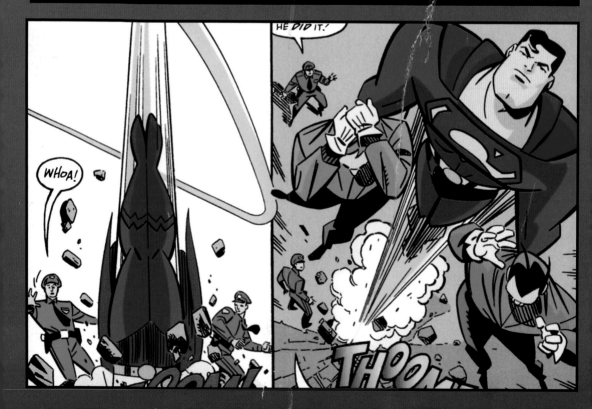

GLOSSARY

abominable horrible or digusting

adjustment small change

authority the right to do something or to tell other people what to do

casualty someone who is injured or killed in an accident, disaster, or war

demonstration display of how something is done

humiliation making someone feel foolish or embarrassed

permanent lasting or meant to last forever

presumptuous assumption of something as true without making sure beforehand

rendezvous agreement to meet at a certain place and time, or the act of meeting someone at an agreed place and time

treason crime of betraying your country by helping an enemy

SUPERMAN GLOSSARY

Clark Kent: Superman's alter ego, Clark Kent, is a reporter for the *Daily Planet* newspaper and was raised by Jonathan and Martha Kent. No one knows he is Superman except for his adopted parents, the Kents.

Intergang: an organized gang of criminals. They are armed with weapons supplied by the evil New Gods from the planet Apokolips. Their advanced weaponry makes them a threat to anyone, even the Man of Steel.

Jax Ur: an evil general from Krypton. Jax Ur is like Superman in that he receives superpowers from the yellow rays of Earth's sun.

Krypton: the planet where Superman was born. Brainiac destroyed Krypton shortly after Superman's parents sent him on his way to Earth.

Mala: a Kryptonian, like Superman and Jax Ur, Mala is given superpowers by the rays of Earth's yellow sun. She and Jax Ur were imprisoned in the Phantom Zone by Superman after they tried to destroy Metropolis.

Phantom Zone: an inter-dimensional prison for superpowered criminals. Those inside the Phantom Zone do not age, and cannot interact with anyone outside it.

Professor Hamilton: a brilliant inventor and scientist from S.T.A.R. Labs.

S.T.A.R. Labs: a research centre in Metropolis, where scientists make high-tech tools and devices for Superman and other heroes.

VISUAL QUESTIONS & PROMPTS

1 Some panels in comics books show two different levels of action. How did the artists manage to get that idea across in this panel?

HOLD THOSE TWO, MALA! I HAVE A PRIZE TO CATCH!

PROFESSOR, GET OUT OF HERE FAST! DON'T LET THEM GET THE MACHINE!

2 How do you think Lois feels in this panel? Explain your answer with details from the illustration.

3 Based on this panel, how do you think Mala and Jax Ur were able to escape their cage?

OH, GREAT-- ANOTHER CASUALTY.

RON, WAIT-- I'VE GOT A JOB FOR YOU.

--BUT A LITTLE SUNLIGHT.

4 Why do you think the creators of this comic chose to change the colour of these panels and zoom in on Jax Ur's face? How does it make you feel?

I SWEAR TO YOU, KAL-EL, WHEN WE GET OUT OF THIS STINKING CAGE, AND WE *WILL* GET OUT--

--WE'LL *CRUSH YOU LIKE A BUG!!*

5 What did Mala do to Inspector Turpin in this panel? What visual clues tell you where her movement started, and where it ends?

WHY, YOU LITTLE FREAK! I'LL GET YOU FOR--

UNNF!

Ha-ha-ha!

THUD!

6 What is Superman worried about? What do you think would happen if others found out about his shrunken state?

BETTER PUT ME IN YOUR HANDBAG.

WE'RE TRYING TO KEEP MY CONDITION A SECRET. IF INTERGANG KNEW ABOUT THIS, THEY'D HAVE A FIELD DAY!

SUPERMAN ADVENTURES